Encounters

Encounters

Alan Walter

Illustrated by Lisa Accadia

First published by Busybird Publishing 2018

Text Copyright © 2018 Alan Walter

Illustrations Copyright © 2018 Lisa Accadia

ISBN 9781925692549

Softcover: 9780648520429

Ebook: 9780648520436

This book is copyright. Apart from any fair dealing for the purposes of study, research, criticism, review, or as otherwise permitted under the Copyright Act, no part may be reproduced by any process without written permission. Enquiries should be made through the publisher.

Images: Lisa Accadia

Book design: Lisa Accadia

Busybird Publishing

2/118 Para Road

Montmorency, Victoria

Australia 3094

www.busybird.com.au

For Kathleen

Where ever you go…

Beginning

Imagine total darkness.
There is no reference,
No time,
No dimension . . .
Just impenetrable black.

The concept of time only has meaning when change exists.
The concept of dimension only has meaning when form exists.

In perfect contrast to this total void of infinite expanse
Is a single infinitesimal point of infinite potential.

All possible light,
All possible time,
All possible form.

Imagine now that infinitesimal point . . .

It exists like a single lonely star
in a night sky,
Whose light emanates from all that is,
To illuminate,
All that is not.
The point erupts,
A sub-atomic explosion.
Streams of light and matter pulse and ripple
from the source of all.
The void is filled.

Space becomes a three dimensional canvas.
Great bold strokes of light and colour,
Galaxial whorls of diamond lights,
Spangled clouds of luminous gas.

Time and form are woven together
to occupy that which was void.
From chaos comes order.
Within order lies chaos.

Observe now this clockwork cosmos.
There is no emotion,
No compassion,
No love . . .

Just pure mechanics.

The concept of compassion only has
meaning when life exists.

The concept of love only has meaning when
relationship exists.

In perfect contrast to this
mechanical
sterility,
Is all encompassing care and
understanding.

All possible emotion,
All possible compassion,
All possible love.

Imagine now that all encompassing care . . .
Its warmth like the sun on an autumn
harvest.
It emanates from all that loves,
In search,
Of that which responds.

Periodic tables coalesce to form
planetary spheres,
Golden suns gently warm mineral
rich seas.

A cosmic pebble disturbs the pool of the
inanimate,

Ripples taking and discarding, forming and
reforming,

As life in all its diversity is catalysed
into being.

Earth becomes a living tapestry.
Vivid coral gardens with splashes of fish,
Majestic forests with surprises
of orchids,

Vast grasslands of wings
and hooves.

Genetic blueprints are refined,
Humanity becomes aware of its
existence.

Out of love comes life,
And from life the choice to love.

And on the seventh day . . .

He waited.

Father . . .

Jesus said we should call you Father.

*You created all that there is.
The very essence of you
is visible to us through your creation.*

The entire universe vibrates in harmony with your tune.

*In a great act of love, you gave us freedom of choice.
The choice to accept and work with . . .
The choice to reject and work against.*

*In Jesus you demonstrate the fullness of your plan.
In Jesus we see a glimpse of your vision for us.
Your Spirit is with us, works through us
in our every response...*

*Every act of compassion.
Every choice to love.*

We pray that we may work for your kingdom.

Come into our hearts and cleanse our minds.

Fill us with your love.

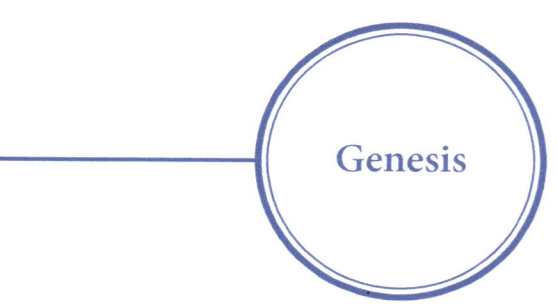

Genesis

The Shepherdess

The day had been unpleasantly cold. On a number of occasions, the rain had turned to sleet and the shepherdess had been forced to protect her face against its icy sting. She was glad of the thick folds of cloth which formed a part of her traditional head attire.

She had first noticed the young couple earlier in the day. They had passed by on their way into town. They were just two of the many travellers caught up in a bureaucratic bungle. Travel in this weather was not by choice; only a remote, impractical bureaucrat would dream up a scheme that required people to travel all over the country at this time of year.

The day had showed all the signs of impending snow, so it would not be the sort of night to spend in an overnight tent. Demand for accommodation was high in the town, and due to their difficult circumstances, the young couple had arrived late in the day, so nothing was available. In any event the prices were such that had there been rooms, the shepherdess doubted that they had the means to afford them.

As a consequence, when they had appeared at the camp in the early evening, and sought the use of one of the rocky caves near her own, she had prevailed upon her husband to give his permission. The caves were smelly but they offered protection from the elements, and the community of animals contributed their body warmth to make conditions some what bearable.

The couple had joined them for a short while at the camp fire and they had shared a little of their stories.

The young man was used to the hard life. He was an itinerant worker who made his living creating small wooden building frames for the traditional mud brick or daub-style constructions. It was this background which had led him to seek this accommodation, for he had spent many a night with the "hill people" while living "on the job" away from his home town. He had been bright and cheerful, but obviously concerned for his young partner, who was pregnant and nearing full term. He clearly felt inadequate at not being able to provide her with a fine room in the town.

They still had that appearance of a newly-married couple, still full of energy and attentive vigour. No one could have guessed that the pregnancy had originally been a source of division between them, for although they had been betrothed, the child was not his. In time, love had triumphed over honour, and he had taken her into his care with a view to marry as originally planned. Now, after some time together, and with her increasing dependence, the young man's love had deepened such that the child would be welcomed unconditionally, with the same love as if it were his own; because it came from her. The young woman was vivacious, and yet innocent, and despite having an air of confidence, the older woman had noticed that she was more than a little uneasy about her time to come. She had told of a recent visit with a relative in the city where she had assisted with a newborn, so she was well aware of the pain and joy that lay ahead of her.

They had talked of family and friends and inconsiderate bureaucrats, and then they had retired early; they had been pleasant company.

It was well beyond midnight when the shepherdess was awakened by the sound of her name being called urgently from outside the cave.

It was the young man, he sounded worried. By the time she had wrapped herself up and answered him, the entire camp was awake. He explained that his young partner was in labour and needed her help. She was a woman of some experience in these matters. The whole group hurried to the shelter and waited outside as the shepherdess and the young man went inside to tend to the young woman.

The clouds of the evening had dropped a crisp layer of snow on the fields and then fled from the sky. Now the sky was crystal clear, and, because the moon had set earlier in the night, the stars blazed all the brighter lighting the fields with their soft light. The anxious group of menfolk paced outside, sharing the burden of worry. The young man felt powerless as he urged, comforted and consoled. He could do nothing to help as his partner cried out, as the birth ebbed and flowed. He had always taken the heavier load, always been the protector and provider, but now he could only be with her.

The shepherdess was calm, as nature was following the timeworn pattern of thousands of generations. The rhythm was quickening now, each cycle of the labour bringing a new urgency until, finally, the young woman gasped and strained and with a triumphant cry, she delivered.

The shepherdess tenderly lifted the newborn child, her weatherworn face glowing with the rapture of the miracle just witnessed. With a splutter and lusty howl, the baby announced his arrival to the world.

The young man wept, overcome with awe at the beauty of the moment.

Outside, the shepherds heard the voice of angels and came in to find…

A babe in the manger.

Jesus, you joined us in this world in the poorest of circumstances, born to an unmarried mother in an animal shelter. Help us to always be ready to welcome you whenever you come into our lives.

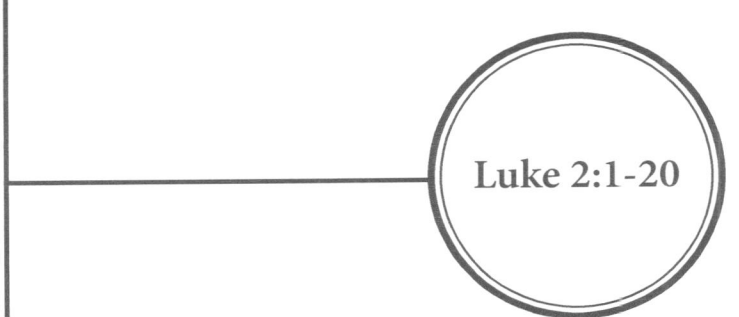

Luke 2:1-20

The Gift

The old man shuffles in.

The familiar stone walls and soaring arches that support the vaulted ceiling are bathed in the soft light of morning.

Several shafts of light play through the rose window high on the East Side of the building.

The rays pick out particles of dust drifting in their path . . . Before splashing across some of the ornate furnishings, and flowing across the exquisitely patterned carpet on the floor.

There is a lingering smell of incense . . .

Over to the side, a number of candles are flickering and sending up tendrils of smoke.

The tendrils gradually disperse as they rise to the ceiling.

The temperature is pleasantly cool, but the day offers the promise of being hot and dry.

The old man looks comfortable here . . .
He is clearly at peace with himself.
He has a look of anticipation on his face . . .

Obviously he has an appointment and he is looking forward to it.

There is a sound . . .

The heavy wooden door at the front is opened. A young couple enters quietly.

The man, in his early twenties, is carrying a small gift.

The woman in her late teens looks shy . . .

But she has a wonderful glow in her face, an obvious inner joy which can't be hidden from the world.

She has a tiny newborn baby in her arms.
The child is silent but looking out of the folds of cloth . . .

Eyes wide in the dim light after the brightness of outside.

The young couple approach the old man who appears very excited.

He hurries to greet them and reaches to take the child.

He has tears in his eyes as he rocks the baby in his arms.

He coos to the child and talks animatedly to the couple.

He tells them of the wonders they have in store.

The couple is amazed to hear all these stories and their hearts glow as they look proudly at their son.

*Jesus, you first revealed yourself as a baby to Simeon in the temple.
Even Joseph and Mary were amazed to hear the prophecy of your life.
Help us to recognise you in the new life which we see around us.
Allow us to experience the joy of Simeon who held you delicate and fragile in his arms.
Come into our hearts like a child enters the hearts of the new parent
and allow us to nurture that love in our lives.*

Luke 2:22-35

Muddy Waters

The river at this point is no more than five metres across. It changes direction sharply, forming a large waterhole with a muddy, sandy beach on the inside of the bend.
The past flood levels are marked out on the banks and in the branches of the trees with ragged bits of plastic . . .
An old tyre . . .
A rusting tin can . . .
Other less visible sins of humanity.

The river continues its mission of cleansing all that it touches.

• • •

The scene is much the same, although in human terms a much earlier time.
There are no ragged bits of plastic . . .
No tyres . . .
No tin cans . . .
Such sophisticated; enduring rubbish had yet to be invented.
But there are other scraps of human refuse.

A broken clay pot . . .
A torn piece of cloth . . .
A fragment of shaped wood . . .
All trapped in the periphery of the river.

Standing knee-deep in the river is a young man in his early thirties.
He is dressed like a caveman, animal skins draped over him,
Roughly pulled in and tied at the waist with a leather strip.
He wears the signs of a hard life.
His skin is deeply tanned and his hair and beard are dark and unkempt.
His eyes are astonishing.
They blaze with an intensity and fervour of one who is unprepared to compromise.

He is speaking to a small crowd . . .
Most are here out of curiosity . . .
Some are here to heckle . . .
Some to listen.

He speaks with a sense of urgency . . .

Jesus, you broke through the wall of fear and chose your destiny.
You left your comfort zone in the carpentry shop and spoke up.
Help us to leave our safe havens and reach out.
Give us the strength and conviction to step out of the crowd . . .
To acknowledge our birthright. . .

Our baptism.

Matt 3:13-17
Mark 1:9-11
Luke 3:21-22

Of the need for a new heart . . .
The need to change to a new way of thinking . . .
A new way of acting.
He urges his audience to come and wash in the river . . .
A sign of a new start.

A young man in the crowd is listening to the firebrand in the river.
He is of a similar age but he has lived a quiet life. He has worked in his father's trade for almost fifteen years.
The words are challenging him,
They pierce him deeply.
He sees that what he is doing is not enough,
The quiet life is satisfying for him,
But he realises that he has become too comfortable,
He is not reaching out.
There is too much suffering being ignored . . .
Too much evil going unchallenged . . .
Too many wrongs not being put right.

At that moment he realises that his destiny is not with his father's trade.

No one else is stepping forward to wash.
It would be so much easier to just join a line,
To do it with all the others.
Why doesn't someone else make a lead?

Why is his heart pounding?
He feels an enormous pressure to stand his ground.

He has had these revelations before,
They are powerful motivators.
He must seize this moment,
Break through the wall of fear.

He looks again at the man in the river,
In his eyes he sees a welcome,
A reaching out . . .
Like an arm to steady his way forward.
His resolve is complete.
He steps out of the safety of the crowd,
He walks, slowly at first, then more confidently to the water.
He feels the weight of fear falling away.
His heart feels like a bird free from its cage.
A surge of power moves through his veins,
He realises now that this is right . . .
This is his destiny.

The firebrand in the river looks shaken, suddenly emotional.
He bows his head for a moment. . .
Then as if spurred on by his own destiny
He pours the water from trembling hands.

As the water is poured, a white bird circles . . .
It glides to rest on a twig near the two in the river.
The crowd looks up . . .
There is a distant rumble . . .
Like that of an approaching storm.

Those who came to heckle saw a bird and heard thunder.

Those who came to listen saw a dove . . .
And heard the voice of God!

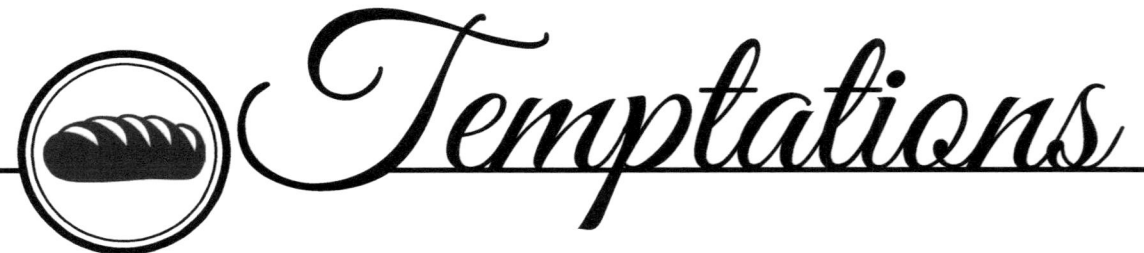 Temptations

The soft light of morning crept into the far reaches of the eastern sky.

The light breeze running before the approaching sunrise felt fresh on his face.

As he watched, the sky was caressed by the first brush of dawn.

Firstly, just a hint of the softest pink, then silently building with bold strokes of the deepest glowing red, before catching alight . . .
Every edge blazing with tongues of fiery gold.

Once again the sun inexorably
hauled itself over the rim of the horizon and began its daily climb upward to its
position of authority . . .

Once again sharing its warmth and light with all that dare to step from the shadows.

• • •

He had been out here on the fringe of the desert for almost six weeks . . .

Living hard . . .
Scraping together meagre rations from the land.
Chilled at night . . .
Parched by day.

His sense of purpose becoming clearer as each day passed.

Life had taken a dramatic turn after his encounter with his cousin John at the river.

He had been challenged to step into the spotlight and accept the mantle of responsibility.

Time and again he had been tempted to walk away,
Take the easy path . . .
Walk back to his comfortable life as a builder . . .

Turning the very stones into bread with the labour of his hands.

He had no major responsibilities . . .
He could just live his life . . .

Play by the rules . . .
Attract no unwanted attention.

Each passing day of his retreat to the desert had cleared his vision. He had come to understand more fully that it was too easy to let life drift by . . .
Too easy not to challenge and right the wrongs within our reach. . .

A man has responsibilities beyond himself.
He is the steward of creation.

He must respond to the intentions of the creator in order to achieve wholeness.

A man cannot live on bread alone.
He must also fan that spark of goodness in his heart until it lights up his whole being . . .

Until it comes ablaze like the sunrise for all to see.

Spurred by this new resolve, he had pondered how he might respond.

As he looked out over the rocky valley towards the spires of the city, he thought of those rich and powerful men who controlled the people with their iron fists.

He thought how different it could all be.
Since his boyhood, he had heard the men of the village describing their dream.

They would rise up under a great leader.
They would forcibly overthrow those currently in power.

They would install a new order, one that was just and benevolent . . .

Was it his destiny to be such a leader?

It was a tempting dream but that was all it was.

For he had seen the corrupting effects of power on men.

He had observed how it seduced the soul, demanding compromise after compromise . . .
Until finally injustice and corruption returned and the very evil, which had been overthrown, once again became the ruling force of the land.

No, to seize power was not the answer.
Tempting though it at first appeared, he firmly rejected the offered cup.

He could not take part in any solution, which placed heavy burdens on people
and crushed them to despair.
That truly was a poisoned chalice.

• • •

As the day wore on, some of the euphoria of the dawn began to wear off . . .
He began to feel inadequate . . .
Daunted by the enormity of the challenge.
As he considered the complex structures and intricately woven interdependencies that protected the vested interests, he began to see where any road to dismantle the system might lead.

It would start out as subtle good-natured, almost bemused comments.

They would paint the challenger as harmless . . . Naïve . . . Eccentric maybe . . .
Not some one to be taken seriously . . .
Condemned with faint praise.

Then if the natural pressures to conform did not have the desired effect, the labelling would take a harder line.

He would be tagged as a dangerous influence . . .
Some one to be avoided.
His character would be attacked;
he would be condemned by association.

When even this failed, the approach would become more overt.
He would be openly challenged . . .
Attempts would be made to trap him . . .
Create an excuse to have him
legally removed.

Finally, when all else failed . . .
When his challenge became too great . . .

They would remove their mask of reasonableness and crush him in a show of naked violence and self-interest.

He would be brutalised and hoisted up for all to see . . .
He would become a sign to anyone who might challenge their power.
He began to doubt, could he really make a difference . . .

How could he be sure?

Should he seek out some sign?

Identify some test, which would give him certainty?

No, there can be no certainty, only faith and trust.

This is the lot of man . . .
He must step into the unknown . . .
He must follow the gentle voice, which he knows to be right.

With that resolution finally clear in his mind and with a clear understanding of where it would all end, he came out of the desert and began to live out his mission
of love.

Matt 4:1-11
Mark 1:12
Luke 4:1-13

Jesus, when you made those decisions in the desert, you faced the temptations that we all face.
The temptation to move with the crowd, to take the soft option . . .
The temptation to seize power, to force our will on those less fortunate or weaker than ourselves . . .
The temptation to hold back or to march to the tune of another's band, and then quickly point the finger of blame . . .
But you chose the path of love despite the cost. And 2000 years later we still celebrate that choice.

The Call

My name is Andrew, I am an old man now. I've long since passed the point in my life where there is more future than past, but I still have dreams, great dreams.

Over these years we have achieved so much, but there is still much to be achieved. That is why I am writing this story.

I am writing so that you might understand the force that has driven this life that I have led.

If I look back on my early life, I see a young man living his life in a fog. A fog of ignorance and unchallenged prejudice. I had never stopped to question the conventional wisdom of the society in which I lived.

I was ready to judge and condemn. So many quick answers . . . So many wrong answers.

Ideas, like the unfortunates of society, or their parents, were somehow the cause of their own misfortune and deserved their plight. Conventions on who one might mix with and who one must avoid. This story may never have been recorded had I not taken a walk by the lake, but that is true of so many things in life. Some call it destiny, some see it as answering the inner call to be. It's extraordinary really, how years after an event, a particular smell or a particular sound will bring a memory flashing back.

I'm sure that we all have decision moments in our lives, moments when we have a flash of inspiration, a sudden understanding of a new possibility. Some times we seize on that moment and take a leap of faith into the abyss of our future, whilst other times we fret and weigh up the pros and cons and finally take a first tentative step. Inevitably, once we start down a new path, our lives are changed forever.

In my case, it all started as a consequence of my fascination for a man named John, who was known as "the Baptiser", that wild man of the river. He was a fiery preacher, fearless in his condemnation of those who abused their power.

I had travelled down to the river on a number of occasions to listen to him. It was on one of those occasions that I first met the man who would so radically change my life.

His name was Jesus, and it was John the Baptiser who first brought him to my attention. He had come forward in response to a challenge to make a fresh start and to undergo a ritual washing in the river.

I will never forget the look on the Baptiser's face as he plunged this man under the water. He knew that this was no ordinary moment. In fact, the whole river seemed to know. The whole place looked pristine and bright as though it, too, had been washed clean and the sun bathed everything with a clear light.

However, I digress. As I said, John the Baptiser identified him as the one who had the answers to my questions, so I gathered up my courage, as I am a shy person, and with Simon my brother, we followed him with a view to finding out more about this new 'guru'.

Well, the first thing to say is that I have never met anyone less fitting of the guru image.

As we were walking after him, he turned and noticed us. He immediately smiled and asked "What are you looking for?".

I blurted out something inane like "Where do you live Rabbi?". I was never good at starting new conversations, especially with someone of guru status. I am not sure what I was expecting, but so often important people have a protective barrier around themselves, and you have to go through the little rituals of bowing and scraping. Jesus couldn't have been more different. He was not the least bit formal. He welcomed us like old friends. Before we knew it we were invited back to his home for the afternoon and stayed for dinner.

He was full of radical ideas, but very different to the angry young men that I had so often come across. So often, their solution was one of violence, solving nothing, just creating greater misery for everyone around them.

Jesus' ideas were much more challenging. He said that in order to stop violence, sometimes you had to take the first blow and not hit back. He said that it was ok to be poor or ordinary, and that we should use the gifts that we have. He said that we should know that God is like a loving Father. He said that we should not worry about our future, that we would always be provided for.

His ideas were so different to the conventional wisdom of the day. It was exhilarating to hear them. After that first meal with him, we didn't see him for quite a while, but the ideas he had expressed were germinating in my soul. I thought over what he had said many times.

It was not until a couple of months later that Simon and

Dear Jesus, help us to have the courage to make you the centre of our lives. Open our eyes to the big dreams, and help us to see the purpose of our lives in your plan.

I were just returning from a fruitless night of fishing, that we saw him again. He was standing on the beach where he had been chatting with a small crowd. When he saw us he signalled that we should cast our nets to the starboard side.

If anyone else had told us to cast our freshly cleaned and stowed nets, I'm sure that we would have kindly suggested that we were the fishermen and that they should stick to their knitting. But Jesus was different, if he said to cast the net, then we would cast the net.

Well, we netted so many fish that we nearly sank the boat hauling them in.

I guess you might say that catching those fish was the turning point for us. We had been thinking about what Jesus had been saying and I guess we caught a glimpse of the future that day.

We saw that his vision was truly worthy. We saw that our lives up to that point had been basically centred around ourselves.

Jesus clearly had a different agenda. He invited us to be a part of something else, he invited us to join him, to be a conscious force for good in the world. His radical view, his sometimes scary view, meant that we would have to consciously choose our opinions, our reactions, our roles.

We would no longer be uncommitted. We would have to start our lives again every day and so we did. We embarked on a great adventure, a new life journey where we were no longer in the centre. We put Gods plan at the centre and did our best to live our lives with that as our guide.

So you see the smell of the sea, the sound of lapping water brought it all back. I remember that day like it was only yesterday, the day that Jesus called me to join him, to give up my life as a fisherman and to become a fisher of men.

It was the start of my real life, my life of living great dreams . . . My life of purpose!

Matt 4:18
Mark 1:16-18
Luke 5:1-11
John 1:35-42

The Cure

It had been a good Autumn. There had been more produce available on the vines and the trees after the harvest than usual. Those of us reliant on gleaning had been able to fill our stomachs on a regular basis. We had also been able to gather some grain from the stubble where the heads of wheat had been missed, so we had some grain for the winter, but we still knew that the combination of cold, hunger and disease would no doubt thin our numbers again.

This coming winter would be my third since I had been segregated from my family and friends. Life had been good to me up until that time. My family, while not landowners, were fortunate to have employment on a large vineyard, and the landlord was a devout man who observed the law meticulously. This included the gleaning laws which now allowed us to survive.

By law, any produce left on the trees or vines after harvest was to be left for those without means. This included anything undersized or unsaleable due to pest invasion, or just missed during the harvest.

My troubles had started simply enough as just an itchy patch of skin on my forearm. Over time it had become deadened and whiter than the rest of my arm. Inevitably, it was noticed and I was summoned before the authorities. Suddenly I was an outcast, no longer allowed to mix with the rest of society. I was forced to join the other untouchables shunned by society. Never again would I be permitted to come in contact with those that I loved…

I was a leper.

Over the past three years more dead patches had appeared on my body and because they had no feeling, they often got scratched and infected, and large ulcers often appeared leaving horrible scars and deformities where they had been.

As time went by, I was becoming aware that my future was limited. I had watched so many of the others die, just shrivelled up. Lack of food, lack of adequate shelter, lack of love, infection, they all took their toll.

I frequently despaired. I was told that this was a punishment, but one that I did not understand. I began to wish myself dead… my misery was so great.

I was at this lowest point when I heard of a new prophet in the district… there had been much talk as it seemed that this prophet taught peace and tolerance… he talked of God as a loving Father.

This was a very different message to the one that I had previously heard. I had received the full force of a horrible punishment from a vengeful God, or so I had been told… but this was a radically different idea. It had changed my whole perspective.

Maybe I wasn't being punished … what if God did truly love me like a Father.

This prophet had apparently said that we should ask the Father for what we needed and that he would give it, in abundance.

In the depths of my despair I resolved to seek out this man and to beg him to intercede for me with this God that he called Father.

When you are healthy it is hard to understand what it is like to be shunned, to be pelted with stones, or hit with sticks if you dared to come near another person. To see the fear and revulsion in their eyes… we were expected to shout as we went about…

"Unclean"…

"Unclean"…

This day I shouted something different… I shouted from the depths of my despair, from the faintest glimmer of hope… I shouted,

"Lord make me clean"

… and he came to me…

he came to me…

people always turned away, but he came to me …

I knelt before him and begged him to make me whole again. I said "If you want to, you can make me clean."

He said, as he touched my festering skin, "I do want to"… and I was made clean. My flesh was healed, but even more, my spirit was healed.

My joy was boundless. The gulf that had been my despair was now filled to overflowing.

I was alive again…

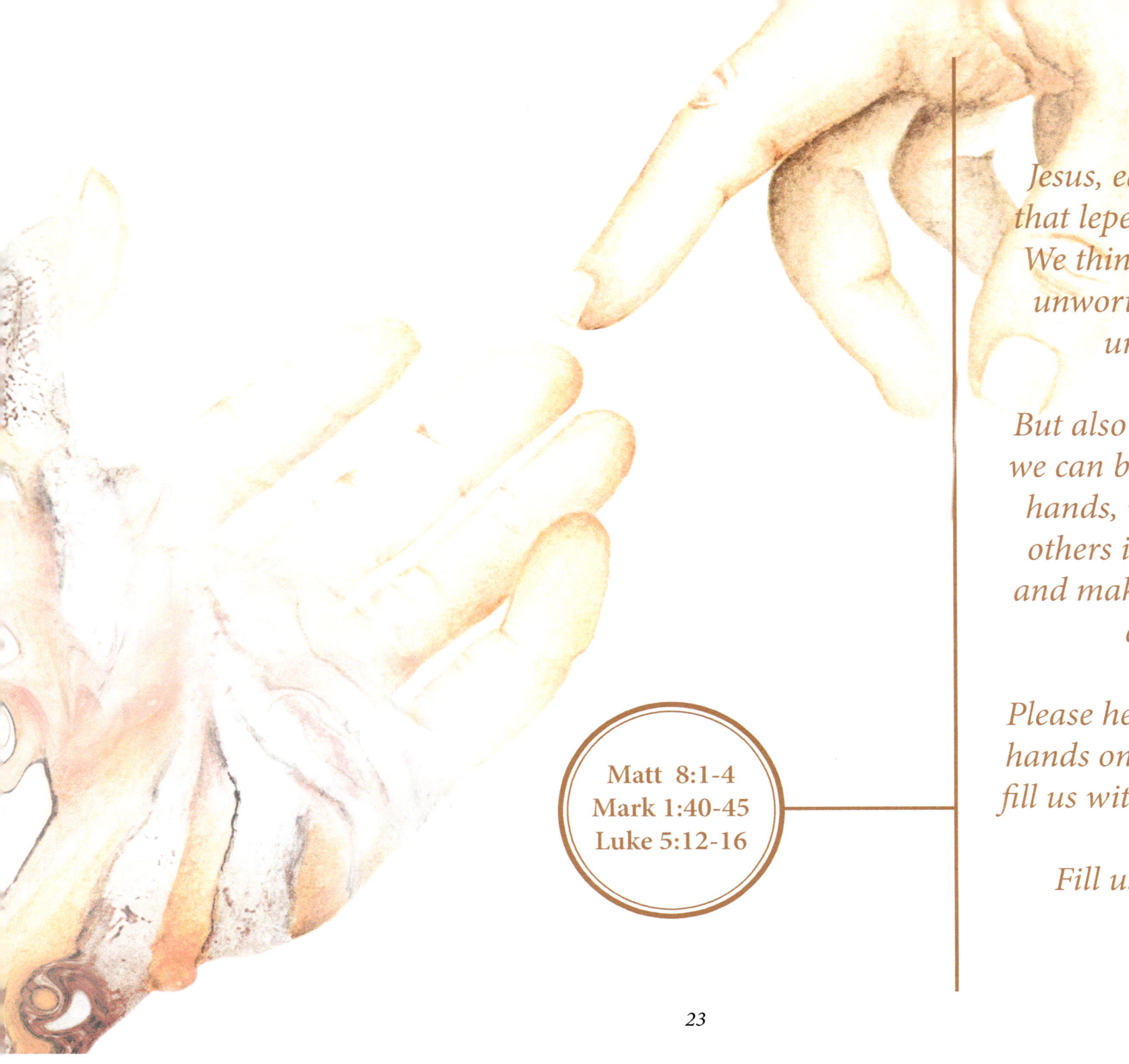

Jesus, each of us has that leper inside of us. We think that we are unworthy, unclean, unable…

But also if we allow it, we can be your healing hands, we can touch others in your name and make them whole again.

Please heal us, lay your hands on us, inspire us, fill us with confidence…

Fill us with love.

Matt 8:1-4
Mark 1:40-45
Luke 5:12-16

Freedom

Twelve years, it had been such a burden.
At times she could barely carry the weight.
The constant attack on her self esteem.
What had she or her parents done to cause this?

While pleasant looking, she was not beautiful.

Within her family she was quiet but not bitter, despite her woes.

In public she was self conscious, some would say downtrodden, but she had a dogged determination which sustained her through her constant illness.

Normally by now, a woman of her age could have expected to be married and to have a young family. Sadly, her condition had prevented any such joys and she kept herself aloof from the attentions of men.

Today.
Today would be different.
Today she would change her life . . .
She had observed him from a distance.
He was a gentle man, and compassionate also. She had seen him in his dealings with others, always warm and welcoming.

He shared what he had and seemed to have a large circle of friends.

He was welcome in some of the best houses but also in some of the most desperate and poverty stricken in the city.

He had made quite a reputation for himself. Some said that he was a troublemaker, a stirrer, a charlatan, a disturber of the peace.

Others spoke glowingly.

Certainly he transformed the lives of those who travelled with him. Rich and poor, popular and abandoned, male and female. Once they joined his circle of friends, they seemed to become energised, invigorated, prepared to stand-up for those who were ill-equipped or too afraid to stand up for themselves.

Within the circle, there was a quiet understanding that you looked after each other without keeping

count, and never questioned each other's right to belong.

She had observed all this, and knew in her heart that he held the key to her future.

Today. Today she must act.

Today she must gather all her courage, put aside all her pride, and approach him.

It had been months. She had thought and imagined this moment many times. She had considered at least a dozen ways to attract his attention.

What she would say . . .

What he would say . . .

How they would meet . . .

Where they would meet . . .

How she would ask him . . .

How he would react!

Every time she thought about it she would lose confidence, her legs would go limp, she would start to fear that her dreams would come to nothing. How could she approach him? She just knew that their destinies were linked. Her moment of truth was approaching, he was just down the road, just entering the village square.

She heard a momentary lull, then a buzz of comment from the crowd of women waiting at the well. They had obviously caught sight of him on the roadway and were exchanging the latest news.

He was on his way to the small open market where the crowds were haggling over their supplies.

As usual, he was with a group of friends, chatting and joking with them, occasionally recognising someone in the crowd and calling a good-natured greeting, sometimes bringing a blush to one of the women embarrassed by his direct and personal manner.

He was quite close now; he was going to walk right past her. She could see his face clearly.

Why was she so afraid to approach this man; he could offer her everything. There was no sign of malice or hidden agendas in his face, his eyes were not veiled, they were clear and sparkling. She could see the glow of an inner life shining out of his face.

She reached out her hand to touch his garments as he brushed past. She knew in her heart that this was all the contact she needed to change her life. She felt a little guilty at her secretive approach, but her years of avoiding men robbed her of the courage to attempt anything more open. She would be satisfied with just this . . .
Just a fleeting touch and be gone.

She had listened over and over to the amazing stories of those who had been touched by this man and she knew that she too could be well again.

At the touch of his cloak she immediately felt a wholeness that she hadn't felt for twelve years. It was like a breath of mountain air, her body suddenly felt well. For a moment she felt euphoric, then despite her initial flush of joy and wellbeing, a knot formed in her stomach, she realised that it was wrong, she had taken something without asking, she felt like a mouse who had found a large nut and was about to scurry home small and furtive.

As she struggled with her emotions, she was startled to hear him speak, "Who touched me?" She felt all the feelings of self doubt and fear come rushing back to her, she had been found out, she felt tears welling up and she flushed red with embarrassment.

Then she heard him speak again more softly, "Who touched me?" and she realised that it was not an accusation she was hearing, it was more an invitation.

Shaking a little, she stepped forward and looked directly into his eyes. Trembling, she told him her story, it all tumbled out, the years of ill-health, her life-force bleeding away every day, the shame and embarrassment, the refused invitations, the years of watching others having normal lives while she stood on the sidelines.

For twelve years, she had haemorrhaged. It had taken a terrible toll not only of her health but also of her spirit. She had become a virtual recluse and now, today, she had lacked even the courage to ask for help, all she had left was a shred of faith that she could be cured, if only she could touch his cloak.

She was oblivious to the others around her now, no longer embarrassed as she told of her secret, broken life. He just listened attentively, sharing her pain as she relived her trials, clearing away her fear with a smile, healing the gaping wounds in her heart with his gentleness, rebuilding her spirit with a joke and a laugh. . .

When she had finished pouring out her story, she once again looked up at him and he reached out, touched away her tears with gentle fingers and told her, her faith had made her well.

She felt swept up, she felt like a tiny two-year-old cradled in her father's arms, she felt like the ten-year-old rushing around the garden with her cousins laughing and shouting, she understood the look in the eyes of her sister at her wedding. Now she knew what it meant to be part of his circle of friends and why they cared so much.

She realised that she had more than her health . . .

She had her life.

Jesus, sometimes we need to be called back into your circle of friends, please reach out and touch us and make us whole.

Amen.

Matt 9:20-22
Mark 5:25-34
Luke 8:43-48

 Man in a Tree

Zacchaeus, why do you run?
Are you afraid of this man they call prophet?

You, who does the work of the infidel!
Do you think he will condemn you?
You should run and hide in a tree!

But the prophet, why does he stop?
Of course, he knows!
This man is tainted,
he works for Caesar,
He fills his belly with the food of the poor.

Zacchaeus, why don't you run?
You must have heard of his rage at the temple.

Aren't you just like those?
Don't you fear his wrath?
You, an outcast, a sinner.

Jesus, this is not a popular move!
Listen to the crowd.
Is this the act of a prophet?
Don't go to his house. . .
You must not eat with his kind.

Zacchaeus, have we misjudged you?
You would give up half of all you have?
You would repay four times any cheating?
This is not the act of one condemned. . .
you, an outcast, a sinner.

Jesus how we misjudged you,
We looked for a mighty king, we found a humble servant,
We expected condemnation, we saw forgivness.

We looked for a man, we found God.

Luke 19:1-10

*Lord, please help us never to judge
the actions of others,
also help us never to put limits on
your redeeming power.*

The Vagabond

Jacob was ten years old, cheeky and streetwise yet still innocent to the worst of the world. He was the only son of a widow, and member of a gang of vagabonds.

Most of his days were spent surviving in the "rough and tumble" world in which he lived. He could regularly be found roaming the markets with the others in his gang, scavenging and stealing.

A date here, a morsel of bread there, in many ways not very different to the sparrows that made their nests in the gardens of the town. He was used to rough treatment, with any adult likely to give him a crack over the ear. Always the ear!

Hitting, twisting, pulling . . .

His mother was a servant in the household of a rich landowner. The very bottom of an intricate web of allegiances, based upon complex power relationships involving crushing debt, fear, and violence.

His father had been in charge of one of the crops, and just before harvest, he had contracted a fever and died very suddenly. Jacob had just turned eight. The landowner had harvested the crop, but never paid Jacob's mother the share that was due to his father.

Her circumstances were such that she had no choice, she had no source of income and had been forced to work as a servant, effectively as a slave in the household.

Jacob's mother could not approach the ower about the unpaid debt, and his relatives had shown little interest in helping, as they themselves lived a precarious existence, only one step away from starvation. They were afraid to intercede for her.

The whole system of wealth distribution ensured that the weak and vulnerable stayed at the bottom of the heap. Only those with family connections or access to a powerful patron on the land, or in the temple, had any surety, and even then there was always someone with whom to keep favour.

Jacob's story was not dissimilar to the others in his young gang. Everyone had his or her own story, it always involved deprivation, and sometimes it was much worse. Through all of this, attitudes were formed and self-images destroyed.

Children grew up to be submissive or angry, and most often bitter or resentful.

Jacob's story was about to change forever. It is amazing how a single incident, sometimes only a few moments of time can have a profound effect on a life. In Jacob's case, he was with the others of his young group, just 'killing time' dashing about making a nuisance of themselves, when they came across a group of adults sitting around apparently listening to a man telling stories.

The storyteller had a weather-beaten face, the face of a man who spent most of his time outdoors. His hair was long and dark and he wore a flowing garment, with long sleeves, tied loosely at the waist.

Jacob stopped rushing about and approached the listening group. He stood behind one of the trees and looked more closely at the storyteller. The eyes of this man of stories immediately captivated him. They flashed with passion and shone with gentleness as the story unfolded . . .

The story was about a widow who was being victimised. Jacob immediately pricked up his ears . . . it sounded like his own mother.

The woman in the story was owed a debt, and had pestered a judge to intercede for her.

Even though the judge was less concerned with justice than the power of his position, after a time he became tired of her pestering and intervened on her behalf.

Jacob was fascinated, he knew that this was only a story, but this storyteller had shown that even an unjust judge could be pestered to provide justice. What Jacob liked most, was that it was a story that showed good triumphing over evil. It gave him hope.

Jacob decided that he liked this storyteller and he waited and listened while the man told other stories. Each one had a positive message and urged the listener to a change of heart, to change the way they lived. They carried a message of love.

When the storyteller finished, some people were taking their children up to meet the man. Jacob moved up also.

Some of the men with the storyteller began telling them to leave him in peace. Jacob's heart sank. He wanted to meet this man. He had even waited patiently, and now some officious helpers were sending everyone away. The storyteller interrupted them and said to let the children come to him.

Jacob's heart leapt for joy. He made his way to the storyteller unsure of what he would say. As he approached shyly, he was startled when the storyteller called him by name. The man seeing his surprise explained that he had noticed him waiting by the tree and had asked one of the locals who he was.

Jacob was stunned. No-one ever seemed to care about him, especially strangers. He was just a kid and most people thought of him as a nuisance. This man was different, he reminded Jacob of his father. He felt safe and wanted.

Jacob formed a friendship that day that was to change his life. He learned to see his life differently, he began to see things from other peoples point of view. He didn't get caught up in bitterness or resentment.

He met the storyteller, and Jesus changed his life…

Amen.

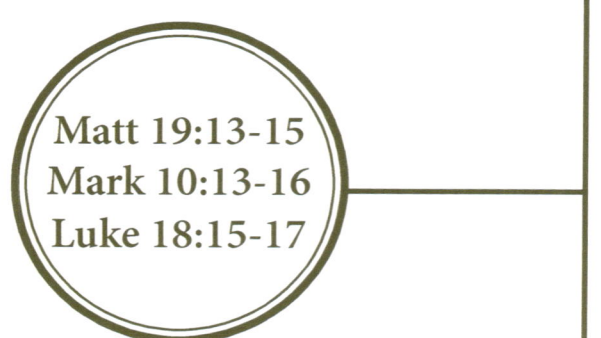

Matt 19:13-15
Mark 10:13-16
Luke 18:15-17

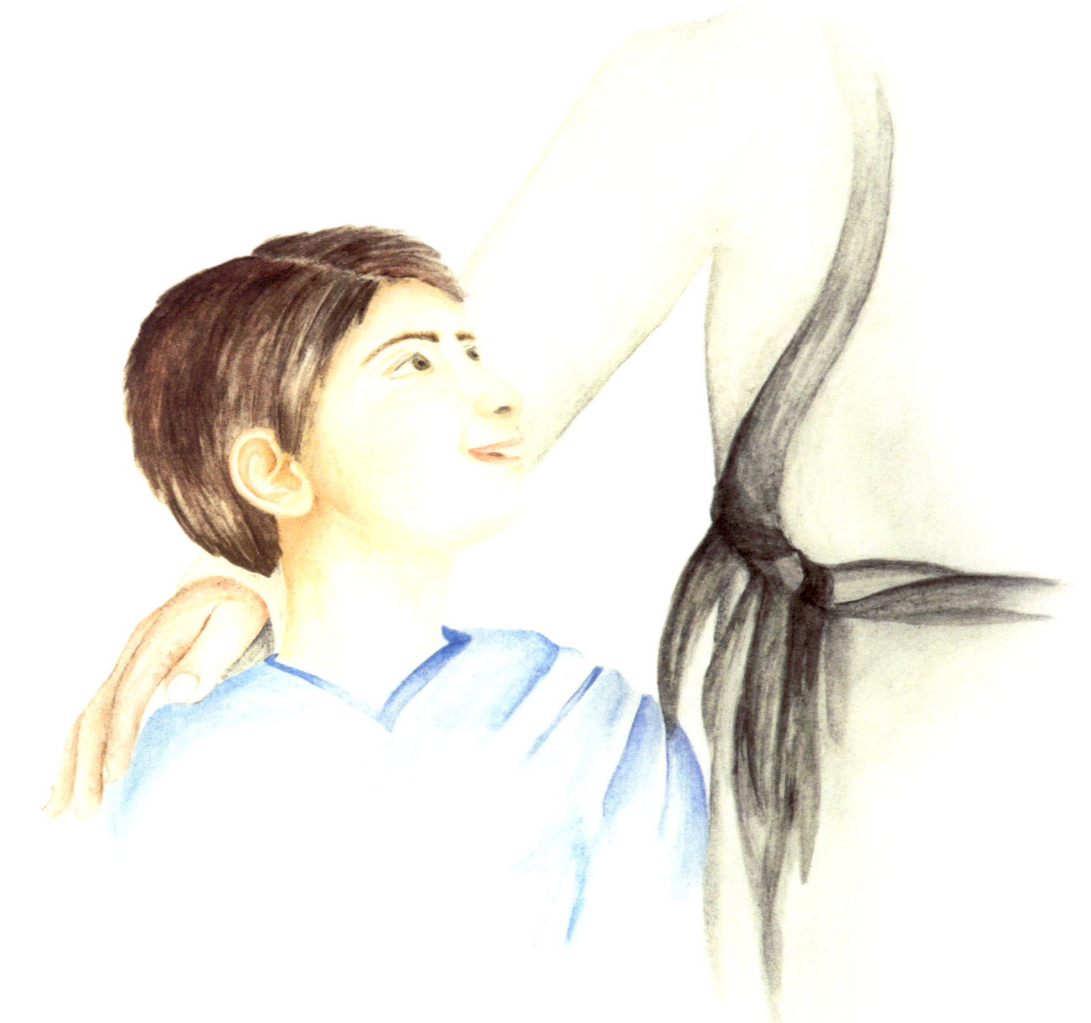

Jesus, you know our stories. You know the path that we have followed that led us to where we are today. You also know the choices that we can make to lead us into our future. Help us to make wise choices and work with you to build your vision for us and for our world.

Victory Garden

Adam, you made your choice,
You chose to live apart.
You pursued that freedom and you found despair.
You should have known that you only had to ask,
It was made for you
This garden,
What will happen to it now?

. . .

The garden is a little overgrown,
It is surrounded by low walls . . .
To keep out those who can't be bothered,
But it is pleasant enough,
A nice place for a night stroll.

Tonight it is clear,
The rising dampness carries with it
The pleasant earthy smell of the fallen leaves
and last summer's grasses.
They are being reinvested for greater growth . . .
Like man's good deeds.

There is a feeling of tension,
Of guarded hope,
The very trees seem to be holding their breath;
A son of Adam is facing a new choice,
Or is it the same choice?
It is a choice of trust,
To stay with the Father though it may cost everything;
The hope and belief that it will all be restored.
The deep love to sustain through the pain.

The choice is made,
Completely alone,
Naked faith,
Adam's legacy is overturned,
Right there,
Right there in the garden,
That was the victory,
For the way of it mattered not.

Father, not my will, but yours be done.

Gen 3:1-7
Matt 26:36-46
Mark 14:32-42
Luke 22:39-46

Jesus, You had the ultimate faith.
You came to understand . . .
That there is no resurrection without the cross.
Give us the faith to recognise and take up our cross
And so share in your resurrection.

34

The Denial

The chill of predawn is beginning to
seep into my bones,
I think I'll move closer to the fire.
What a night!
A man has some pride!
What was I supposed to do . . .
Stand back and do nothing?
Especially after all that talk of leaving
and then questioning my loyalty . . .
In front of everyone!

We could have taken them,
Hit hard then run . . .
That's the tactic!
But no . . .
Play the pacifist, take it all on
yourself!

He can be so infuriating at times.
I know that they will lock him up,
Certainly beat him . . .
But he doesn't want my protection,
He knows best!
"What's that?"
"No, I don't know the man!"

*Dear Jesus,
when we are angry
and upset, our pride
can make us
hurt those we love.
When we are afraid,
we may lie to protect
ourselves, but we
lose our integrity.
You know our frailty,
you were a man but
you broke through
those barriers . . .
Please help us to be
true to ourselves,
true to you.*

I don't know why I should get dragged into this now, best to act dumb.
That girl at the gate was a close call,
Trying to get me involved . . .

I don't like the feel of this whole business.
These people are really nasty.
Someone said they are going to bring charges . . .

This is getting really serious!

If they recognise me,
I'll end up taking a beating too!
I don't quite know what went wrong? Last week we were heros, now look at us!

"Look, half the guys around here have an accent"
"I seem to have told everyone else a round here . . ."
"I don't know him!"

Why, did I say that?
He's worth a thousand of them.

I wish I had a tenth of his courage,
He will never step back from his principles.
Huh! Dawn already!

Hey, they are bringing him out!
My God! What have they done!

Don't look at me like that . . .

My God! What have I done . . .

Matt 26:57-58, 69-75
Mark 14:53-54, 66-72
Luke 22:56-62
John 18:15-18, 25-27

Pilate

What is truth?

It was more of an accusation that a question…

And at that point, I wasn't really seeking an answer.

In any event, the answer would have been incomprehensible to me.

My world was a house of cards, a finely balanced arrangement of brutish force counterpoised with deadly fear …

A world of flattery and cunning deception.

I was powerful, have no doubt, and that power was definitely of this world, but it came at a fearsome cost…

The price of failure was not something to contemplate.

Those who ruled over me were even more ruthless that I…

And those who coveted my position were ever ready to cast me aside and take my place.

You see, I was the governor of a tiny province in the Roman empire, a province called Judea…

I am known to you as Pontius Pilate.

The fact that I so famously asked that question "What is Truth?" revealed the cynacism that had taken hold of me. I had seen enough to no longer hold any romantic notions of truth.

In my life it was a "dog eat dog" world and for this brief moment in history I was head of the local pack…

Power in my world was not conferred, it was always taken.

There may have been some elaborate ceremony that dressed it up and gave it a sense of respectability, but rest assured that such ceremonies were always after the sometimes brutal struggle of greed and naked ambition had taken place.

The search for truth was not something that occupied my time to a great extent, but I had certainly started out with the sense of righteousness and firm belief that comes from being sure that you are right…

After all, the Roman way of life offered many benefits, often deposing tyrants and removing despotic regimes.

However, I had observed over the years that the population in general did not appreciate the finer points of Roman rule, and in my more reflective moments, I recognised that the average citizen saw little difference. Their lives remained a struggle to simply survive and our Roman tax collectors were just the same local thugs answering to new masters.

So, my cynical question, "What is Truth?" I certainly didn't know, and was too self-absorbed to await the answer…

But the mind is a strange thing…and mine, having formed that question, even as cynical as it was, would not let it lie unanswered…

Over the years it stayed with me…

Just as the events of that infamous day stayed with me…

The man, to whom I posed it, had amazing quiet strength, even in the face of death.

Here was a man with a mob screaming for his death by crucifixion, a man already scourged and brutalised by my soldiers…

Men are normally either fiercely defiant with that crazed look in their eyes, or completely terrified and emotionally broken…

But this man was completely rational and resolute…

His emotion appeared to be not fear but deep sadness…

I still remember his eyes… an incredibly open face… a deep well of sadness!

I glimpsed for a moment the look of a father whose children had failed him…

A man whose friends had all deserted him…

A giver of gifts whose gifts had all been rejected.

But for all that, I also saw the face of a father who still dearly loved his children…

A man who still loved and missed his friends…
A gift giver who would continue to give…

For a brief moment of time I understood some of the sadness that I saw in those eyes…

At that point, I wanted to free him, but in reality my power is only an illusion and the crowd was at the point of riot…

I was just a fearful man out of my depth being swept by the tide!

It was not for many years that I finally began to understand some of what I saw and heard on that fateful day.

For truth is not in the power that we gain over others…

Truth is not to be found in the possessions that we amass…

Truth is not in the oratory we may speak…

I had to lose all my power and most of my possessions in order to finally see that truth is ultimately to be found in relationships…
We have to forgive like that ever-loving father…

Love our friends even if they turn away…

And keep giving even if our gifts are rejected.

For to love and to be loved is the ultimate location of truth.

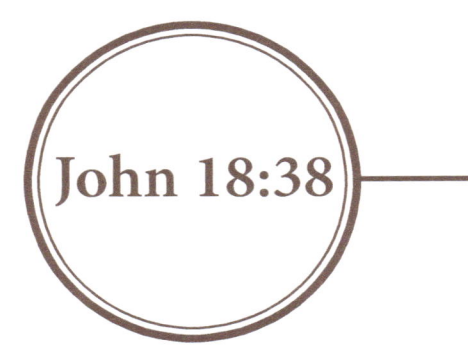

John 18:38

Jesus, you showed us truth,
You showed us that we should touch those we can reach,
Look into the eyes of those who look at us,
Share of the gifts that have been given to us.

Each of us carries that weak, fearful Pilate within us…
But we also walk with you, and you are:
Ever ready to forgive…
Ever ready to challenge…
Ever ready to love

Simon

My day started out like just so many others before it.

I had risen early because of my planned trip to town...

I had to take a couple of animals to the market.

My son Rufus had collected together a few figurines that he had carved from a piece of driftwood. He often came home with pieces that he found by the lake.

He spent much of his leisure time whittling and carving his little figures with considerable imagination.

Rufus really has quite a talent, his work always fetching a good price from old Thomas in the market.

My other son Alexander had stayed over with his cousins after our families had shared the seder meal the night before.

We regularly spent time with my brother and his family...

Especially on festive and solemn occasions.

So I left Rufus with his mother and traveled to town with just the animals for company.

The weather was fine, but there was a sense of tension in the air.

Spring days often have a hint of thunder about them and this day was no exception.

I had obtained a good price for the animals, and was just heading up to visit old Thomas when I heard a commotion coming towards me down the roadway.

I looked up to see a group of soldiers hustling three men up the road toward me.

Each was carrying a heavy beam of wood across his shoulders.

They were being treated brutally by the soldiers: dragged by their shackles from the front, clubbed and prodded from behind.

They were being followed by a jeering mob that seemed to be aiming their venom and abuse at the first of the three unfortunate men.

My first thought was to make myself scarce, but I was tranfixed.

The leading prisoner had tripped and fallen under the weight of the beam.

As he was hauled to his feet, a group of women, totally distraught, their faces torn with grief, ran to him from the crowd.

They seemed completely oblivious to the soldiers . . .
To the rain of blows . . .

They helplessly pulled at him . . .
Pleaded for him . . .
Cried for him . . .
Could do nothing for him . . .

One of them managed to wipe his face with a cloth for just a moment. He looked at them.

Bent almost double under the weight of the beam, He managed to raise a hand,

Brush just one face,
Just one touch. . .
Then they were roughly thrown aside,
Soldiers shouting,

Beating,
Whipping . . . As I stared, rooted to the spot,

my heart aching for him . . .
For them . . .
I had never before witnessed a moment so tender, such hurt . . .

Such love. . .

I stood there shaken, overcome with the depth of the emotion that I had witnessed.
Next moment, one of the soldiers grabbed me and propelled me into the centre of the group.
I was jolted from my trance. . .
Fear gripped my heart, they would take my life just for the sport . . .

They dragged the beam off the shoulders of this amazing stranger and forced it onto me.

As I staggered under the weight of the beam, I turned momentarily and caught his gaze . . .

It was an exchange that I will never forget. I understood so much from that look . . .
It burned into my very core.
I lost my fear.
I hoisted my burden.

I suddenly knew that I had a tiny part in an incredible drama that reached far beyond this moment . . .

Far beyond this place.

I knew precisely where this road led.
I had seen so many take it before.

It led to an excruciating death . . .

But I had glimpsed something more in those eyes, something beyond the pain . . .

Beyond death . . .

And the beam felt like a feather.

Matt 27:32
Mark 15:21
Luke 23:26-34

*Jesus, when we truly meet you,
you take away every fear,
you lighten every load . . .
Help us to see beyond the moment, so that
any cross we may bear
becomes a feather.*

Amen.

The Tree

The scene is one of absolute freshness;
the leaf mulch on the hillside is deep and
well-composted.

An earthy smell rises from the damp,
and the morning air still has that fresh dawn
chill.

The spider-webs are like a galaxy of stars,
a myriad of dew drops glistening in the
brightness of a new day. Beneath the top layer
of mulch, a mighty struggle has been taking
place, a tiny seed has swollen and thrust out
a tendril of green, and has burst through the
surface unfolding to produce a single pair of
life sustaining leaves.

Nearby in a small animal shelter, another
struggle has been taking place. With a lusty cry,
a new born baby announces its arrival to the
world.

The air is filled with the sounds of creation.
Plants and animals form the tapestry,
man steps back and looks in wonder.

Time has passed.

A sturdy young sapling now stands
where the first tendril of green appeared.
Already the sapling is part of the mesh of life,
contributing its leaves back to the soil
and supporting a world of creatures under its
young bark.

In its branches is a tiny nest; A mother bird
watches expectantly as a young finch
balances awkwardly on a twig, preparing to
make its first flight.

Nearby a child is reunited with his parents
after wandering off, a first step towards
independence. The child had been gone for
several days.

The air is filled with the sounds of
development and growth.

Creatures relax in their garden of Eden as
mankind struggles in the world of his creation.

Time has passed.

A magnificent sycamore tree now stands on the hillside, it is tall and straight, its branches are strong and it has a large canopy of shiny, fresh, green leaves which have recently unfurled after the spring rains.

The sunshine of the late spring day is warm and a light breeze shimmers the leaves. It creates an inviting dappled shade under the tree.

Nearby, a man is seated on a rock surrounded by a large group of friends. He is speaking of a better world, a world where every man has a right to live life to the full. The crowd are in rapt attention as they glimpse a vision of what could be.

The air is sweet with the smell of spring. There is a feeling of harmony and good will.

Man is momentarily in God's kingdom.

Time has passed.

Something is very wrong.
A group of men are hacking into the tree.
Each blow of the axe bites deeply into the soft
green wood, the tree shudders with each blow.

The birds and animals who drew life from the
tree have scattered and are afraid.
Finally with a loud crack and a groan
the tree crashes to the earth.

The men look upon their work with a grim
satisfaction.

Nearby an innocent man has been stripped
of his clothes and is being whipped.
He has done no wrong, but the crowd have a
blood lust, and they are out of control.
The man is brutalised and abandoned.
His friends are in a state of shock,
they are too afraid to intervene.

The air is filled with the smell of fear.
The feeling is one of crushing violence
and despair.

Mankind has chosen the path to evil.

Time passes quickly now.

The destiny of man and the tree have come together. The man is whipped and beaten and forced to carry a large beam hewn from the tree.

Finally in an act of ultimate violence, man and tree are brutally united with nails joining flesh and wood, and thrust into the air as a grizzly sign to those who believed they could create a better world.

And at the third hour,
Life-force finally drain from man and tree.

. . .

The air is still.
All creation is in shock.
Man looks upon the results of his inhumanity.

Time passes.

Nature steps in and binds up the wounds of the tree.
A sprig of green has appeared from the base of the stump.

Birds and animals return to the area with new hope, as once again they may shelter in the branches of the tree.

Nearby, a large rock lies cast aside from an empty cave

. . . and two men finally understand the truth.

The air is filled with the sounds of new voices, speaking of a new world, a new vision, a new hope, a kingdom of mutual love and respect,

. . . of resurrection.

Matt 1-28

The Road

The road is not truly a road as we consider one of today, it is simply a meandering patch of bare earth through the grasses of the early summer.

The grass is short near the path where the animals have stopped for a momentary nibble, but taller with long seed heads of the wild rye and barley further from the path.

There are no fences near this path, there is no need, all animals are carefully tended in small flocks and everyone knows the rules!

The path is flanked by an occasional boulder and small gorse bushes abound. The land is still untamed, only the people are tame.

As we come around a small rocky mound, we see a stranger resting on a large flat rock, he seems to be waiting for us.

He smiles and hesitates as if waiting to be invited.

He is dressed in the fashion of the time, and his hair and beard are like everyone else's, rough cut with a knife sharpened on stone.

We greet him in that self conscious, guarded way that unsophisticated people of the land greet a stranger.

He stands and smiles a warm twinkling smile and gathers us with a simple gesture of his hand.

He is obviously comfortable with our kind of people, and we immediately feel warm and relaxed with him.

He is so unlike the local leaders of the town. They are familiar with power and have that hard edge which is so crushing to the rest of us:

they rule with fear,
they control our lives,
one word of theirs we could be
shunned, forced to live alone.

They have the ability to strip us naked in the crowd, make us the laughing stock.
We know that they are prepared to go much further than that.

Their greed for power and control will take them beyond what we are prepared to endure, so we keep our eyes downcast and live by their rules.

But this man is different:
he doesn't demand submission,
he seems to enjoy our spontaneity,
he urges us on to our dreams,
he empowers us.
We can sense in his presence that same sense of a father watching his children develop and grow in a safe environment which he has created and maintained for them, not restricting but gently urging, always allowing that spontaneous growth while gently pruning.

As we walk with this man, we become more aware of the good around us.
We feel the warmth of the sun,
smell the wild perfume of the grasses,
and we feel that we could forgive those who so recently kept us shackled,
for we begin to understand the depth of their fear, the emptiness of their lives.

They are in a cold dark place, but this man, he lights a fire and invites us into the circle.
We are near the village now and we have a sudden realisation that this man wants to go on.

We aren't ready to leave his company.
We take a risk and invite him to stay with us.
We are in a moment of panic, but he smiles and we realise that he already knows us so well. We feel self-conscious but he immediately waves that away.

Of course he'll stay with us.

We rush around and fuss making the meal and once again we relax in his company,
timidly, we invite him to say the blessing over the meal.

He takes the bread
and breaks it
and blesses it.

He takes the bread...

We suddenly realise that He will always be with us, we recognise Him.

He is the one they tried to break, to crush.
He is the meek one who inherited the earth.
He has mourned and been comforted.
He has been humbled and has emerged exalted, and He continues to work for peace.

Jesus please be with us on our road to Emmaus.
Help us to see you in all people.
Help us to welcome all who we meet on our path,
as you welcomed all on yours.
Amen.

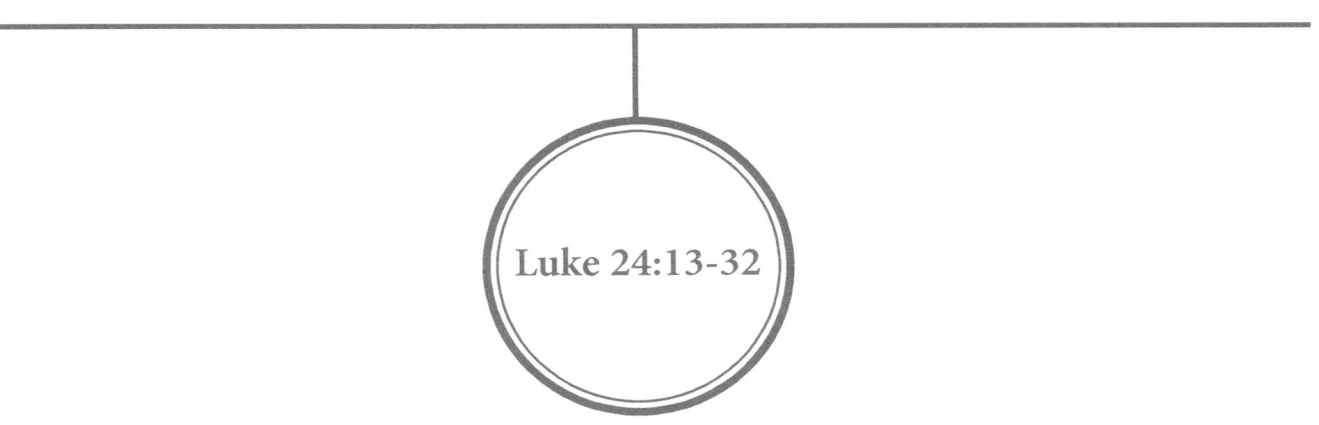

Luke 24:13-32

www.ingramcontent.com/pod-product-compliance
Lightning Source LLC
Chambersburg PA
CBHW050854010526
44107CB00048BA/1605